How to Retain Talented Employees

ASHFAQUE AJANI

ISBN 10: 1717279619
ISBN-13: 978-1717279613

DEDICATION

Its dedicated to the leader of leaders, True Leader IMas.

JNKsa & SFZsa

This publication is designed to provide accurate, helpful and informative material regarding the subject matter covered. The suggested tools and strategies covered in this book may not be suitable to everyone, and are not guaranteed or warranted to produce any results.

This book is sold with the understanding that the author is not engaged in rendering legal, financial, accounting, or other professional advice or services. If legal advice or other expert assistance is required, the services of a competent professional should be sought.

The author does not take any responsibility for any liability, loss or risk, personal or otherwise, which is incurred as a consequence, directly or indirectly, of the use and application of any of the contents of this book. The names of the persons appearing in this book have been changed for privacy reasons.

The author does not take any responsibility for any liability, loss or risk, personal or otherwise, which is incurred as a consequence, directly or indirectly, of the use and application of any of the contents of this book.

CONTENTS

Introduction -

This small book is written with an aim to guide Hiring Managers, Recruiters, Recruitment Managers, HR Managers, Heads, Directors to retain their all the employees including Top performers.

We understand the problems, challenges faced by Employers - In fact in every era the biggest difficulty is to retain its valuable assets i.e. Good performer & talent employees. Hiring emotionally intelligent staff.

Hiring good talent may be sometime easy task but keeping them is another big challenge for HR Managers.

There are plenty of excellent opportunities are easily available in the market today, employees are aware about such prospects, if they think they can find something better then would find it simply.

A good amount of investment is put in to hire a good resource but when he moves, all the efforts, training, time, plans goes waste. The purpose company hires HR expert to ensure such talented people are retained but How to do it. So here are some guidelines, steps, processes for you to work and accomplish your task and prove your capability to the management.

What will you gain from this book

You are supposed to do some activity every month and on all single day. Main goal is to make your people happy and make them feel proud of the brand. As said this will not happen in a night, continuous efforts required, thought process. I assure you after reading this book, you will be able identify the problem of high attrition in your organization and will gain How to Retain employees creating unique solution yourself.

So, let's begin....

Why Business face challenges to retain its staff?

C hallenges for business is to attract and retain qualified staff & it's more challenging for startups and Small Business, there has been many failed attempts to start a small business that failed simply because the owner could not get, and keep, good help to work with him.

Among the various crafts and trades this may not be much of a problem because the craftsmen generally know the other craftsmen of the same craft that are in the same general area. A bigger problem might occur when the business may need more specialized skills that may be hard to find. the solution to this is to consider the staffing needs ahead of time and ensure that there is a sufficient pool of workers to be able to maintain an adequate stall or postpone any attempt at start up until you can be confident of having the people needed to do the work.

SME's do not have a budget or ability to pay compensation as large organizations.

They could not incur high volume of money on advertisement, to promote brand which do not attract candidate to attach himself with them.

Big firms face same kind of problem due to plenty of job opportunity available in the market.

Management must put some thought over it and executive some friendly benefit programs to hold its members.

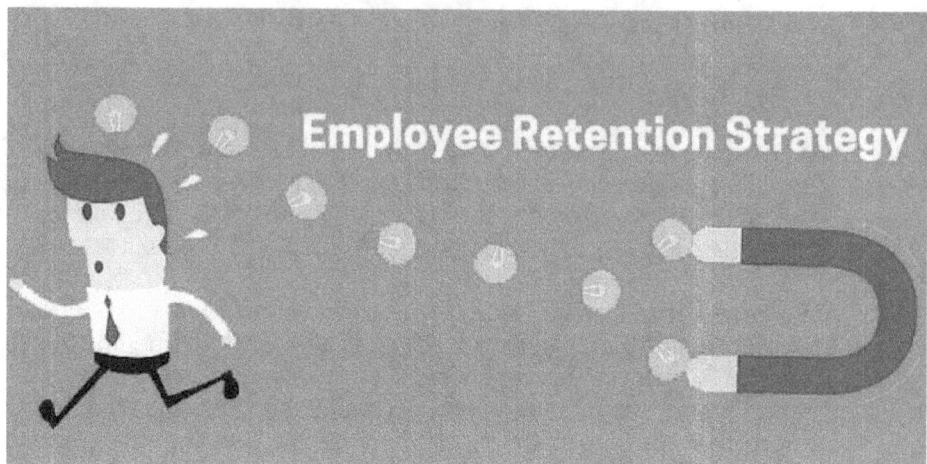

Why retention is so important?

Do you agree finding right talent for right job is not an easy task? If your answer is positive then you got your reason of retaining.

Many companies are now beginning to view employee retention as a critical issue. High employee turnover increases expenses and can also have negative effects on company morale.

Implementing strategies devised to retain good workers can help counterbalance replacement costs and reduce the indirect costs associated with high staff turnover such as lost clients and loss of morale. Employee retention has become an important topic for many reasons.

These include:

Social media networking tools such as LinkedIn make it easy to observe new job opportunities or get poached by another company.

Costs associated with hiring new staff, advertising, interviewing and hiring etc.

Training new staff

Loss of productivity. It can take up to 2 years for a new staff member to reach the same productivity levels as existing staff members.

Loss of engagement. Retained employees who see a high turnover often get disheartened and lose engagement.

The longer staff stay with an organization, the more productive they get. They get to know the systems, products and learn how to work together as a team.

Many high performing companies have loyal employees and each company has its own strategies for retaining their employees.

Some of the interesting things to consider:

Compensation is a factor but does not play as big a role as you would think. Over-compensation will not offset a poor work environment

Job fit is significantly important. Hiring the right people for the right positions by realistically advertising job positions will save you a lot of trouble in the long run. If you oversell a job you can suffer from high staff turnover. Effective retention strategies often begin during the employee recruitment process. Employees are more inclined to remain with a company that fulfils the promises made when their employment offer was extended. Companies that provide a realistic view of their corporate environment, advancement opportunities and job expectations to new hires can positively influence employee retention.

The work environment and culture matter. Staff want to feel appreciated, comfortable and included in their place of work. Employees that enjoy what they do and the atmosphere in which they work are more likely to remain employed with their company.

Implementing an employee retention program is an effective way of making sure key workers remain employed while maintaining job performance and productivity.

Most prosperous organizations are those that respect their employees and invest in building an engaged work place environment.

BECAUSE IF YOU LOSE BEST ENGINEER OR SALES PROFESSIONAL THEN YOU WILL NOT BE ABLE TO EASILY REPLACE THEM. IT IS AN INABILITY TO QUICKLY REPLACE LOST EXPERIENCED, TRAINED AND KNOWLEDGEABLE EMPLOYEES THAT CAN SERIOUSLY DAMAGE YOUR BUSINESS. ESPECIALLY IF THOSE THAT LEAVE YOU JOIN ONE OF YOUR COMPETITORS. SO VERY IMPORTANT TO HAVE RETENTION SURVEY PRACTICE TO LOOK AT THE REASON WHY EMPLOYEES LEAVE COMPANIES AND SO IT'S IMPORTANT TO EXECUTE SOMETHING TO PREVENT IT.

Why do you think employees leave?

Some of companies have high attrition rate %.... any idea why?

The main reason is Job satisfaction. Employees should know what is expected of them, not only day to day, but in the overall strategy of the company. All employees should have goals and the means to attain them. Without that motivation to attainment then the job can become mundane, and alternative offers can become attractive. Employee participation in company policy is always useful in reinforcing their perception of their worth to the company.

The poor quality of supervisors and line managers are another reason for a lack of employee retention in many companies. Too often promotion is given to those who have shown a flair for the job they were doing, but cannot manage. There is a world of difference between a great salesperson and a good sales manager.

Until more companies become more professional in the way they manage and motivate their employees, those who fail to do so will have a low level of employee retention and so struggle to compete against those more professional in the way that treat and motivate their employees.

Replacing an executive can cost 2 or 3 times their annual salary.

When Human Resources are trained on how to recruit the right employees and Supervisors are trained on how to appropriately manage the intellectual capital in an organization these groups together can significantly reduce employee turn-over and make a significant positive impact on a healthier bottom line for the company!

Importance of Customer

Before we understand why it's so significant to retain employees let's understand the Importance of our Customers which will give you a bigger picture why and how we can reduce employee attrition.

Any business person can, and should, tell you that the customer always comes first. From management and ownership to sales associates, the idea of customer service is key to effectively contributing to a good business.

Customer fulfilment comes from the key idea that "the customer is always right". But fulfilment for the customer goes beyond being right. It stems from the satisfaction of being treated properly, finding goods and services relevant to the needs of the customer, and having an overall positive and informative experience with any business.

One important aspect of customer fulfilment is to earn the trust of your customer or client. This ultimately begins immediately upon meeting the client or customer. A friendly, sincere greeting ensures the customer feels welcome and appreciated upon arrival. Going beyond a simple "hello" or "What can I do for you?" is very important. Learning and remembering your customer's or client's name assures the person they are significant to you. Using their name repeatedly (but not TOO often) in a conversation shows the customer that you are catering to their individual needs.

It helps to ask specific questions such as "I see you are viewing this product; what information can I give you about it?" or "What will you be using this product or service for?" To truly fulfil the needs of the customer, you must view the customer as someone you genuinely need to satisfy. Make it your personal goal to learn as much information as you can about the customer, their expectations, their concerns, and what they want to gain from their experience with your business.

Some may wonder why all of this is important though. Imagine a customer walking into a business. Upon walking in, he isn't greeted by the workers. He is not offered help, though he has many questions about an expensive product he would like to purchase. Because he is not offered help, he is dissatisfied with the store and leaves. This business has not only lost a sale, but a potentially loyal and valuable customer. In addition to that, he is likely to share his negative experience with family and friends. This potentially takes away more customers from the business.

However, what if he had a different experience? Imagine he goes to another similar store, and is greeted with a warm hello and questions about his needs and interests. The workers make eye contact during the conversations and seem genuinely interested in his needs. He gains a sense of fulfilment and satisfaction with the service he receives. He purchases a product from the business, and leaves the store very content. It is very likely he will return to the store because he had such good experience. In addition to that, he will likely recommend to others that they go to this business.

Overall, customer fulfilment is essential to the success of any business, big or small. By being customer-appreciative and customer-oriented a business is sure to do well and keep their customers fulfilled and returning for more.

Importance of Employee

Imagine that you have open an excellent school in your area which is better in all the aspects like world class education system, books which are written by renowned authors, PHD's, top most infrastructure facility, high standard security system, reasonable fees and all admissions done for every class but you do not recruit Teachers / Professors or your teachers are leaving from the current setup. Now what, where do you find your business. Lost.

Understand here the importance of your precious resource. You will be ready to hire new staff at double the prize to run the business.

On other scale if you have the required number of teachers but they are disinterested and unhappy with their work, their discontent could destroy your school and right education will not be transferred from teacher's desk to students and a big loss to the society and nation.

Same case is when your customer wants to order to you to buy services and products, but your important employees in the department or in that case your sales team is demotivated, will you be able to do business with customer NO.

As like customer even your internal staff is at same importance and is an asset. therefore, treat them as you want your customer should treat you. You put efforts to earn customer trust, don't you think wining employees trust is same important? As already read in previous section that when customer was given respect, attention & was happily welcome, He gained sense of fulfilment and satisfaction with the service he received, so why employees are not treated with same gesture, attention, if you do then believe me your employees will do everything for you and for your customers, they will stretch themselves and service to your customers even if require going off the way in an appropriate manner. If you believe that customer brings business to you then you are wrong, it's your employees who do the business for you, retain customers for future business.

Happy employees will talk the benefits of your services, products & solutions and passionate in dealing with people. These group will ensure customer satisfaction and engage customer to be memorable because the focused is on wellbeing of the organization, yes, these are your loyal staff. High morale employees will increase revenue double as compare to average individual, so here is the opportunity to work on employee and win customer satisfaction, higher the volume of happy staff higher the chance of retaining customer. So, thing about it.

Case study: Harvard Business Review: The Impact of Employee Engagement on Performance

While most executives see a clear need to improve employee engagement, many have yet to develop tangible ways to measure and tackle this goal.

However, a growing group of best-in-class companies says they are gaining competitive advantage through establishing metrics and practices to effectively quantify and improve the impact of their engagement initiatives on overall business performance. These are among the findings of a new Harvard Business Review Analytic Services report of more than 550 executives around employee engagement research that features in-depth interviews with 12 best-practice company leaders.

The report survey found that many companies find it challenging to measure engagement and tie its impact to financial results: fewer than 50 percent of companies said that they are effectively measuring employee engagement against business performance metrics such as customer satisfaction or increased market share. But one group of companies—called "high prioritizes" in the study because they saw engagement as an extremely important priority—are effectively using metrics and shared some best practices for tying engagement to business performance.

These   include:
■ Avoiding rote surveys. Leading companies devote significant resources to carefully crafting employee engagement surveys so they ask pointed, clear questions that go beyond measuring "satisfaction." They then pore through the data to find the hidden stories of what's working and where there are pockets of dissatisfaction. Finally, senior management uses this information to inform strategy and policies going forward.

■ Ensuring that goal alignment is occurring at every level of the organization and is well-communicated. Top managers set and communicate business objectives; middle managers are responsible for creating specific objectives for employees that support broader business goals; and employees are given the tools to succeed, some autonomy, and accountability to meet tangible goals aligned with corporate   goals.

- Using data to leverage engagement initiatives to improve performance, typically customer satisfaction/net promoter score (NPS)surveys and feedback, and then tying winning results to recognition programs to reinforce alignment and the activities linked to performance.

In most companies, today's leaders are acutely aware that there is much to be done to ensure that they have a focused and highly engaged workforce. Connecting engagement to business performance requires considerable effort and top management focus—and, to a large degree, it is about how you do it. But there is enormous opportunity for companies that get it right.

The most common measurements best-practice companies are using to connect engagement to business performance were those that tied customer metrics with engagement metrics. Specifically, many best-practice companies interviewed found NPS and the service-profit chain to be powerful tools to link engagement initiatives with business goals.

Employee Happiness: after all, it is the customer who has chosen you for your unique skillset for your expertise and for your business. However, without happy employees you will not have satisfied customers. Failure to do this can even cause greater dissatisfaction in the workplace.

How to Retain talented employees? Or Reason for leaving organization

Do you really accept that employee leaves the organization …… think about it? The simple answer is NO. you know why even after leaving the work place He is still attached & connected with them. He follows company on social media, keep update himself on progress of the organization and takes out the information from his ex-colleagues who are still working. Then a question, why he left. He did not leave the company but he separated from his boss. Yes, it's true usually because their managers chase them away. It doesn't matter how great the company is, what are all the benefits and perk. If the immediate boss / manager lacks the necessary skills to manage his employee effectively. Its high risk the performer will leave, only top performer no even average performers and below will think of same decision, because respect is something every individual expect and requires.

So, what to be done – Train your managers, leads, supervisors first to handle the juniors, how to lead their subordinate because their success is linked and dependent on their team, if team is unsuccessful then outcome will be the same. It is no importance how much you spent to recruit most talented individuals for the job.

Employees may have initially joined the company because of the generous nature of their pay package or the perceived reputation of the organization. But the duration of their stay and the quality of their work will be determined by their relationship with their immediate supervisor.

The essence of great management lies in addressing each employee's needs in a way that enables them to build a strong and vibrant work environment.

How should they do this?

Does the employee know what is expected of him or her? –

if not then talk to them immediate and understand what they would like to do, what is their core area which interest them and are passionate about. If their interest contradicts with the roles, responsibilities decided for them, then quickly align in such a way that both party's employer and employee's need is fulfilled.

Do they have the necessary tools and materials to do the job?

If not then as manager provide them all the necessary resource to do the work.

Do they have required skills to accomplish task if not then arrange a product / process training for them.

In real terms does their manager care for them?

Is there a framework in which the employee is encouraged to develop and is there someone who cares enough to encourage this development?

The manager's role is to identify and release the unique talents and skills within each employee and help channel these to the good of the company and individuals. Only by identifying the employee's talents can the manager achieve the company's goals and satisfy client's needs.

How can this be applied in an organization's day-to-day business?

Focusing on the employee's strengths helps them find the right fit within the organization. After all, the best salesman does not necessarily make the best sales manager.

Employees leave primarily because they are unhappy in their jobs and their managers lack the skills necessary to address their needs. An organization can retain talent by ensuring that everyone has the right tools, knows what is expected of him or her, enjoys the work, is recognized for his or her achievements and is encouraged to develop his or her career.

Section B - How to Retain talented employees? Or Reason for leaving organization

The attitude around here is that the floggings will continue until morale improves.". taking an example of an old-line manufacturer, was facing many problems. They had a militant union, managers were being forced to work long hours, burnout was high and turnover was constant.

"We are the meat on the sandwich." he further confessed. "Below us we have staff who could not care less what we have to say and above us we have management who has no idea what we do." Despite some of the best wages in their industry, this company was dealing with high sick leave and was struggling to retain good people.

Everybody knows the data. Boomers are retiring, there are four generations in the workplace and there is a shortage of talent. This is becoming critical in all sectors of the economy, especially the public sector, where there are strict limits on what people can be paid. So, what do people want? How can you attract and retain the best talent, especially if you are limited in how much compensation you can offer? Before we answer these questions, take a moment and think about yourself. You are the very person that any organization would want to keep.

You have a choice between 2 employers. Organization 1 offers you a great environment. You are respected and are given flex time when you need to handle personal matters. You believe your work has meaning and your opinion counts. Organization 2 is very negative, full of unbending rules and unwritten norms. Nobody really cares or wants your ideas and your peers see you as a threat. The only advantage Organization 2 has over Organization 1 is that they are willing to pay you $10,000 a year more. When you answer that question for yourself, then you will understand from a deeper level.

So therefore, what else can be apart from paying high salary?

Solution #1: Pay employees fairly and well ... then get them to forget about money.

This solution is in 2 parts. The importance of the first part is that if employees believe they are unfairly paid, they will be demotivated. They'll complain, goof off and eventually quit.

And, in fact, most employees (not necessarily yours) don't believe they're paid fairly.

But, assuming that wages are competitive and fair, studies have shown that pay has no impact on retention or on productivity. In fact, focusing on pay can denigrate performance.

So, the second part of our guide is: then get them to forget about money.

Don't bother coming up with complicated incentive pay programs, particularly if they pit employees against each other. Such programs just get in the way of employees focusing their attention where it should be -- on doing a good job!

Solution #2: Treat each employee with respect. Show them that you care about them as persons, not just as workers.

According to a study one of the things employees most want is: Sympathetic Help on Personal Problems. Today, this probably would be called something like: Sensitivity to Work/Life Issues. It's even more significant to today's employees. Small-business owners and even HOD's can do much to treat employees with respect and increase productivity.

'RESPECT EVERYONE THEY DESERVE IT'

Solution #3: Praise accomplishments ... and attempts

Praise accomplishments using positive feedback, more than anything else, employees want to be appreciated for the work they do.

And not only accomplishments, but also good attempts; just as you would, if you were training a young child.

At least four times more than you criticize, which, for many of us, is in the reverse proportion to what we tend to receive.

Do it promptly, as soon as observe. Praise delayed is praise denied. Don't wait for the annual performance review. If possible present him a small gift to feel him good even if its cost of small keychain or pen. Not necessary always but sometime yes, but with words always.

"A person who feels 'appreciated' will always do more than what is expected"

Do it verbally and in writing. And putting it in writing does not have to be time-consuming. For example, use your business cards. When you catch someone doing something right, briefly note what they did and how you feel about it. Sign it and hand them the card.

Do it publicly and in private -- based on both the magnitude of the accomplishment and the personal preferences of the recipient. Not everyone is comfortable with public praise.

And do it sincerely. If right after being praised, you were asked to do a favor, would you feel appreciated ... or manipulated?

One of the way to respect someone is to listen him carefully when he is talking to you because he considers you worthy to solve his problem if in case you cannot personally aid him directly then refer him to someone who can be helpful. (Covered below in detail)

Solution #4: Clearly communicate goals, responsibilities and expectations. NEVER criticize in public -- redirect in private.

You can implement this by using something called constructive feedback, as you will see, constructive feedback clarifies expectations, provides information, and, done right, is not criticism (even in private).

Solution #5: Recognize performance appropriately and consistently

On the one hand, reward outstanding performance, e.g., with promotions and opportunities.

On the other hand, do not tolerate sustained poor performance. Instead, provide coaching and training. If that doesn't work, relieve them! This may sound obvious, but studies show that most employees don't believe that poor performers are dealt with effectively.

Solution #6: Involve employees in plans and decisions, especially those that affect them. Solicit their ideas and opinions. Encourage initiative.

Employees want to feel in on things. Do yours? They can, if you solicit their ideas and opinions, using the inquiry skill. Listen them.

And encourage initiative. All too often, employees who rock the boat or stick their neck out by expressing creative ideas are slapped down, rather than rewarded. Don't let that happen at your workplace.

Solution Tip #7: Create opportunities for employees to learn & grow. Link the goals of the organization with the goals of everyone in it.

According to the study, most employees are lukewarm about promotion/growth opportunities. So why is learn & grow a top ten tips?

Well, the Study examined how employees choose employers. Of the 16 factors studied, advancement opportunity was ranked at the bottom, but gain new skills ranked toward the top. Some of your employees want to climb the organizational ladder. Virtually all your employees want to learn and grow.

This certainly includes formal education and training programs. And: OJT (on Job Training), special assignments, projects, coaching and mentoring.

And link the goals of the organization with the goals of everyone in it. Every employee should be clear how the work they do contributes to your organization's mission ... and to themselves.

Solution #8: Actively listen to employees' concerns -- both work-related and personal

An individual manager must listen to his employees & can be learned about the active listening skills... Here is what an entire corporation has done:

International Telecom company's 'Individual Dignity Entitlement Program' requires managers and supervisors to meet one-on-one with each member of their staff every 3 months. They discuss the employee's answers to 6 questions about how they are treated. Then action plans to address issues are created and the progress toward previous action plans reviewed.

Solution #9: Share information - promptly, openly, and clearly. Tell the truth ... with compassion.

How do your employees find out what's really going on? Via the rumor mill? Or from effective and trusted communication programs?

And, if layoffs or benefits cuts are in the works, let your employees know about it and help them deal with it.

Solution #10: Celebrate successes and milestones reached -- both organizational and personal. Create an organizational culture that is open, trusting and fun.

Birthday parties are an obvious example of celebrating personal milestones (and having fun). Here's an example, which combines the organizational and personal:

The signatures of all 48 employees who worked on that first Macintosh computer (not just Jobs and Wozniak) were moulded on the inside of the product's case. Can you imagine the pride those employees felt then ... and today?

Post your intelligent people testimonial / view on company's website or in authorized doc what they feel good about company. Why not even photograph. think about it.

So, concluding this chapter here with what we discussed.

People leave bosses and not organization.

Managers must actively plan career path for his subordinates.

Money is not only gain, but employee needs more then it to be in any organization.

Pay employees fairly and well.

Treat each employee with respect.

Praise accomplishments ... and attempts.

Clearly communicate goals.

Recognize performance appropriately and consistently.

Involve employees in plans and decisions.

Create opportunities for employees to learn & grow.

Actively listen to employees' concerns -- both work-related and personal.

Share information.

Celebrate successes

*there are couple of more such tricks or activity which can be implemented to retain employees like providing other benefits, organizing picnic, hygiene food, Gym / yoga - corporate wellness program
counselling, etc. but these addition to what we discussed above.

Section C - **How to Retain talented employees? Or Reason for leaving organization**

Throughout learning

Work/life Balance policies

Benefits

Ownership

Mistakes are acceptable

Be friendly

Go out of Lunch

Don't be inspector

Flexibility

Throughout learning:

Create a "Desire to Learn"

The most effective training is delivered to trainees who are motivated and interested - who have a "desire to learn." In most cases, new employees do come to you with that desire. They're fresh. They're motivated. They want to succeed in their new position. But what if you're re-training an employee for a different position? One that he/she may not necessarily be interested in? Or what if you're training an employee on technology that he/she is intimated by? These situations can create anxiety and hamper the effectiveness of training.

How can you create a desire to learn? Here are some tips:

Listen to the employee's concerns. If you can understand - and address - the employees' worries and insecurities about training, you can remove a significant barrier to learning.

Provide examples of specific, tangible ways that the training will help the employee.

Involve the employee in establishing training objectives, timeframes and methods (more on these later).

Focus on "development" not "remediation." Nobody likes to feel that they're inadequate or lacking in critical skills and knowledge needed to perform in their jobs. But many people can be motivated by the prospect of developing new skills and abilities. Do whatever you can to avoid making trainees feel "incompetent" or "stupid."

Choose the "Right" Training Method

People have different learning styles and preferences. Some people read the instructions first, others refer to the instructions only after they've tried to "figure it out" on their own. Some prefer theory; others hands-on application. To the extent that you can (obviously it can get expensive to design individual programs for every employee...) try to match training methods to learning preferences of employees.

Work/life Balance policies:

Maintaining a work life balance is essential if we are to be effective and fulfilled in life. It is easy to lose focus when we are out of balance. Work-life balance is now considered to be the second most important driver in employee attraction and commitment ahead of compensation. Importantly, those workers that have it work twenty-one per cent harder.

The preoccupation with work-life balance is no surprise in today's busy existence. Gone are the days when leaving the office meant leaving work behind. Blackberries, laptops, iPhones and the magnitude of social media sites mean our availability and our access is constant. This easily to respond optimistically to work-life balance or the ups and downs in life whilst others are not. The good news is it can be learned with a little bit of discipline.

gets out of control, particularly if you are a type a personality (workaholic). The competitive global environment and current economic uncertainty puts increasing pressure on people to work overtime due to cuts in manpower and the constant threat of redundancy.

The consequences of all this, not surprisingly, is more stress, ill-health and in-balance. We have better living standards and more wealth than ever before yet people feel less happy with their lives. Women especially have greater opportunity, achievement and more influence and financial independence yet face increasing levels of depression.

Every human being deserves the right to live in balance giving time and energy to the things that enrich and fulfill us and make our lives worth living. Positive psychologist, Martin Seligman writes that some people are hard wired.

Benefits:

Over the years, one of the most important factors candidates cited in searching for employment was benefits. Surprisingly this was second to salary. Considering the high cost of healthcare and prescriptions, benefits have played a vital role in the way people look for jobs. Unfortunately, in recent years, we have seen a decline in the benefits being offered. Companies are finding it difficult to keep pace with the rising costs of insurance and other employee benefits, forcing them to either reduce or eliminate their offering.

Many believe that employees are entitled to benefits, feeling it is the company's responsibility to offer some level of support. Others believe that employee benefits are a privilege not a right. For this group, they believe that any offering is better than nothing at all. Adding further fuel to this hotbed issue - the number one reason that people file for bankruptcy is medical bills. So, what is the truth about employee benefits - is it a right or a privilege?

Let's begin by addressing the many inaccuracies and misconceptions relating to employee benefits. Myth: For Only large companies are required by law to provide benefits. Truth: The truth is that while some benefits are mandated, the majority are not. Standard benefits such as healthcare, holiday pay, and vacation are routinely offered by companies of all sizes as part of a benefits package. While most companies do offer some or many of these benefits, from a legal standpoint, these "benefits" are not actually governed by the law.

In a competitive marketplace, employee benefits can be the deciding factor for many candidates. Organizations offer these benefits to attract and retain high quality employees. Business owners know that providing perks to employees is a worthwhile investment to attract a higher caliber of employee. Therefore, while the company must spend significant money to provide this type of coverage, they do so as an investment to growing business, and attracting and retaining a talented workforce not because they are required to do so. Today's world is highly competitive. Individuals who have graduated with a BA or even MBA usually only work for top companies. This means that for small to medium size organizations to compete they must find creative ways to make the opportunities more appealing.

Ownership:

Make employee owner of his work, here I mean give him freedom to take his own decision, let him take risk and manage the work as per his convenient, because if you consider him only as worker, then you can't expect him to do wonders for you. But when you make him feel the owner of the organization or his work then there are high chance of producing more results because now his mindset has change and he started looking as things as its own. He will ensure everything is perfect including his own behavior, in short, its change of mind.

Mistakes are acceptable:

Learn from your mistakes, as a business leader, it's found that one of the scariest things to do was to give your people the freedom to make mistakes. While mistakes allow individuals to learn and grow, they can also be very costly to any company but calculated one will not. How, good leader is one who allows employee to take risk & own decisions even sometimes it results in loss. But by doing this you are helping to grow and preparing him for future. 'Mistakes are acceptable but doing nothing is not at all acceptable'. As a leader you must be very clear and allow them to do by own, make yourself available for them to guide, mentor and transform your knowledge on daily basis. Understand one can only learn from a mistake after one has admit he has made it. If you educate him to accept his mistake rather than blaming to management or team members, colleagues for insufficient support then result will not be as expected. But by accepting mistakes the possibilities for learning will move towards growth.

Be friendly:

Friendliness is about approaching others and being approachable, how many times as a boss we are approachable, understand there is difference between available and approachable. For e.g. my boss is available whole day in the office but as an employee I do not wish or like to approach him. But on other hand even if he is traveling I would prefer to disturb and check I can use his lunch box, use his laptop, or take leave or in that case to find a solution of my problem, as far as your team is approaching you for all support then be assure things are under control, you know why because they consider you as a mentor, Leader and had built trust in you, they have a hope. But if on other side of table if they keep distance from you and had a limited official relation then this is a concern area. Immediate you need to take things in your control.

Go out of Lunch:

Yes, not a bad idea, ask them to arrange and organize lunch for whole team and join them. This will create a trust between you as a boss and your team staff. The most important way to foster understanding is to plan activities that will get people talking to each other in an informal atmosphere. Get your employees talking to each other about their cultures by organizing "cultural" pot-luck lunches where employees bring in ethnic foods and share recipes.

At your lunch employees from different cultures can share photos and tell stories about their lives. You can even have a separate lunch for each culture represented at your workplace. Eating and sharing information about different cultures leads to understanding, acceptance, and friendship.

Don't be inspector / be Flexibility / provide WFH

Having a flexible working arrangement which allows employees to sometimes work from home can be beneficial.

The traditional model of having everybody clock in at nine in the morning and out again at five had its advantages, but it reflected a mindset which has long had its day. Some firms, of course, have taken longer to emerge from that mindset than others, but recent years have seen a substantially more adaptable approach on the part of many bosses as the lifestyles of employees as well as consumer expectations change.

It would be better to understand how a Friend differs from a Boss first. A friend is one who is showing love, affection, passion, and care. Even when you do anything wrongly, a true friend will support you and be on your side, since friendship forgets and forgives everything. If you want to be a good friend to your subordinates, inevitably you must adjust with and accommodate errors, lapses, and lack of interest in the workplace. Boss" means one who gets the work done.

So be a friend don't be an Inspector.

Voice in the organization:

This might have been covered indirectly that let employee feel they are ambassador. The day they start observing that they are not heard by the senior management things will start rotating opposite side. An international automobile organization setup their manufacturing unit near country. Everything was going well as per plan but when survey was done its found that their skilled workers are unsatisfied which is impacting on overall productivity. Later found the reason of their sadness that they did not had any voice in the organization & were struggling for all small benefits. So, it's very important to have a feedback mechanism to allow employees to vote and share their concerns. This will help to reduce attrition and engage them for long term employment.

Family   friendliness:
Family-friendly benefits include life insurance for dependents and flextime which lets employees select their work hours within limits

Retirement and financial planning:

Employers offer several types of retirement plans as well, so this could be one of the best benefits you can think for your staff.

Educational assistance:

Offer undergraduate & Graduate education, most of companies have sponsorship policy, employee's fees are sponsored by employers either for higher education or enhance skills competencies.

Monetary bonuses:

Overall, 63 percent offer some form of incentive bonus plans--60 percent offered the plan to executive employees and 47 percent to non-executive   employees.

Mental and emotional health: Employee assistance programs (EAPs)--providing confidential counselling to help employees with problems that may distract them from their work--are offered by 73 percent of respondents.

HOW TO DESIGN REWARDS AND RECOGNITION PROGRAMS THAT IMPROVE EMPLOYEE ENGAGEMENT AND RETAIN TALENT

Survey of over 800 HR Executives published by Human Resource Executive Magazine in August 2010, 46% of executives indicated that one of the biggest challenge they face is ensuring employees remain engaged and productive.

Best practice research indicates that organizations that reward and recognize their high performing employees have significantly higher employee engagement and achieve their business objectives.

Key principles to guide the setup of reward and recognition programs

The following are some of the principles that should guide the development of an effective recognition program in any organization:

Recognition awards must be linked closely with the organizations' business plan, culture, values, leadership principles and business results. Understand the factors that affect your organization's strategy

Teams or units that foster diversity and inclusion, and innovation should be weighted high in selection for rewards and recognitions

Must be communicated well to employees and managers at all levels. Evidence points that organizations that communicate programs well have employees who are more satisfied than those who do not

Establish a reward mix that aligns with behaviors that support your organization objectives

Programs should offer rewards that are meaningful and flexible for employees

A variety of awards should be offered and for large corporations with multiple business units and locations, there may be corporate and divisional programs with large annual awards at the corporate level, and small on the spot business specific awards at the divisional and locations levels

For an effective recognition program for a large company there must be a balance between centralized to decentralized structures for the administration of the programs. Decentralized structure for the business level and location that are tied into a centralized corporate program. On-line administration of any recognition program is highly recommended

To ensure that managers are not restricted in the usage of the programs, budget should be centralized. On-line training of managers in the selection of employees for awards should be mandatory and usage may be tied to a manager's performance

A significant omission in most reward and recognition programs that could negatively affect team building and performance is to base awards only on individual merit. Corporate level awards should have a reflection on the immediate teams of the corporate award recipients by way of team awards

Establish a credible evaluation process. Employee feedback on the operation of the reward program is key for improvement and acceptance by employees

Motivation

how to motivate those who work for you is something that everyone needs to learn if they want to be a success in any industry that they are in. The people that work for you and the ones that make your product and/or provide the services that you are selling so make sure that they enjoy what they do and they will do it that much better. Sounds pretty simple huh? Well, it is and you can learn these things in just a little bit of time. You would be surprised to see what a difference these types of tips can make to your overall company performance.

By taking the time and energy to motivate your employees you will find that not only do they work better for you, they are happier as well. Proper motivation means teaching people about themselves and what they want to get out of their lives. Your motivation will teach them what their own personal goals are and how they can achieve or even exceed them with ease. This is a great service that you will be doing them and your company. You will find the money pouring in when you do these types of things and that is always a good way to run a business right?

No matter where you live you can find some great motivational workshops that are set up specifically with the employee in mind. These are group activities that you can get everyone who works for you into. They are usually quite fun and the employees will not ever have to pay for them. They are getting free lessons on how to live more happy and healthy both physically and emotionally, it is perfect!

Talk to some other businesses in your area and see what kinds of motivational services they have used in the past and how much they cost. Take the time to search out the very best motivational speakers as these will give you the best course for your money. They can change everything, even the home lives of your employees. The more innovative the ideas that these motivators have the better they may work. Don't let yourself be boxed in by expectations, think outside the box and let the imagination soar. Be willing to try new things with your employees and watch things get better and better in the workplace.

We know that the ultimate responsibility for motivating employees lies within the individual employee. We know that both the meaningfulness of the work and the work environment itself can have a sizable impact on employee motivation. We know that intrinsic rewards and motivators tend to have a much longer lifespan for employees than extrinsic rewards and motivators. And, we know that what motivates one employee will not necessarily motivate another.

But sometimes a little knowledge can be dangerous. What do I mean? I mean that knowing what motivates employees is only half the battle. The real test is our ability to create a culture that fosters high morale and motivation. Too often we fall into the trap of incorporating the latest and greatest motivational programs in hopes of creating improved performance. These short-term remedies can often serve as band-aids to problems that require much greater attention. As a result, improvements in morale and motivation tend to occur sporadically within an organization instead of in a collective, synergistic way.

The solution is an integrated approach. What is needed is an organizational-wide, integrated approach to creating a culture of high morale and motivation. What is needed is a top-down management philosophy and corresponding strategies that integrates management practices with efforts to enhance employee motivation. What is needed is greater consistency throughout the organization in communicating to employees about performance standards, expectations, feedback and professional growth opportunities, to name a few.

Why is integration so important? Without an integrated approach to creating a motivated workforce, inconsistencies will surface throughout the organization and quickly sabotage any positive momentum that occurs. For example, a high performing supervisor will quickly lose her motivation if she keeps getting her decisions overturned by her respective manager. A great benefits program will do little to motivate employees if the tension in the office is so thick that you could cut it with a knife. An awards luncheon will send mixed messages if employees are expected to pay for their own lunches. A supervisor who preaches value-added customer service and then yells at his employees will quickly lose respect as well as the value-added customer service that he so desires. In each of these examples, there are contradictory messages that ultimately will serve as de-motivators and most likely lead to employee apathy.

How Google LinkedIn works

Valued   **workers**

When Google went public in 2004, a letter from the firm's founders was sent to investors, outlining the firm's modus operandi. Co-founder Sergey Brin added the following: "Our employees, who have named themselves Googlers, are everything. Google is organized around the ability to attract and leverage the talent of exceptional technologists and businesspeople. We have been lucky to recruit many creative, principled and hardworking stars. We hope to recruit many more in the future. We will reward and treat them well."

A simple question

Only a few years ago, the main challenge of getting a job at Google wasn't the competition, but the now-abandoned bizarre interview questions posed.

Explain a database to an 8-year-old in three sentences
This challenge aimed to test candidates' ability to boil down concepts to their constituent elements, and relate them clearly and succinctly

Why are manhole covers round?
Aspiring Googlers were asked this question to test their logical reasoning skills, as well as their ability to think flexibly about problems and solutions

How many piano tuners are there in the world?
A classic Fermi problem, this aimed to test practical estimation and the ability to work confidently with numbers on a large scale

How many times a day do a clock's hands overlap?
This question was a more straightforward test of applied mathematical ability, but could still throw the unprepared

At Google, employees are considered the company's most asset – the backbone of the organization. They are given freedom, a healthy work-life balance, incredible perks, and even the chance to have fun at work. There are many who have a view point that its waste of money and time & may find them simply absurd. And yet, the results speak for themselves.

Given that Google is a relatively young company, its rate of exponential expansion since being founded in 1998 illustrates just how effective this fresh method of management is. Google's exceptional success shows how far a company can go when it celebrates and nurtures its staff, rather than considering them replaceable tools. "What HR should and must focus on is understanding the relationship between the things which motivate and engage people as individuals", says Laurence Collins, Director of HR and Workforce Analytics at Deloitte. "The environment, work, growth, reward and flexibility it offers, [are] part of the employee proposition."

"Job perks are an important part of some organizations' value proposition, and the more quirky or unique the better", says Thompson. Google certainly has quirky and unique perks down to a tee, such as providing napping pods and hammocks for workers to rest when needed, which can boost cognition levels and reduce stress. For a subsidized price, employees can also visit on-site masseurs to relax and minimize work-related back pain, while doctors are available throughout the day for other ailments too. Comprehensive health plans include dental and optical care, and, more unconventionally, alternative medicine and even fertility treatment. When the time comes that a Google baby is born, $500 is gifted to the new parents – just because it's a nice thing to do.

Innovation, communication

Google considers enhancing collaboration to be one of the best means for facilitating great work and innovation. Managers encourage their team members to communicate and spend time together as much as possible, for bouncing ideas off one another is how the magic often happens. Within the office space, departments are grouped together by glass dividers, which enables frequent idea exchange without disturbing others, while also maintaining an open and illuminated environment.

Another concept that the people operations team has implemented to inspire the next big idea is '20 percent time'. This programmed allows employees to work on a personal project outside of their allocated duties for up to 20 percent of their working week. Although one day a week may seem like a lot of time to divert from one's responsibilities, it is during these hours that an individual's passion and ingenuity is best harnessed. Illustrating this point are the products that have been created from personal projects, such as Gmail, Google Talk and Google News.

"Google is really good at providing job enrichment. Googlers are assigned several projects at a time and have ownership of their projects. They work on these projects from beginning to end, so they are involved through the whole process and are able to see how their work makes impact on the organization", says Dr. Jonathan Booth, Professor of Organizational Behavior and Human Resource Management at LSE.

Each employee is assigned their own mentor within the company. Naturally, the mentor is chosen based on data that matches the compatibility of the two individuals. The 'career guru' program allows junior staff members to discuss their career development, daily schedule and how to deal with office politics, within a confidential and friendly environment. "It is a great place to work because it is a learning organization", says Booth. "They really focus on learning and development." Staff members are also given the valuable opportunity to ask senior management any work-related questions they wish during sessions called TGIF (Thank God, It's Friday), which, in true Google fashion, often take place on Thursdays. "Our weekly all-employee meetings started when 'all' of us amounted to just a handful of people, and continue to this day even through we're now the size of a respectable city", writes Bock.

Then there is the Google-O-Meter, which allows staff to vote on employee suggestions to gauge their popularity and whether each policy or perk has enough traction for implementation. "Googlers have a lot of voice mechanisms in place, so that their opinions and views are heard", claims Booth. As illustrated by such policies, communication is key at Google. Giving personnel a chance to speak up not only fosters a productive work environment; it can also lead to significant changes within the business.

LINKEDIN

it was the spring of 2015 and LinkedIn's technical teams were feeling the heat. Competitors were aggressively recruiting engineers and too often the managers and leaders only learned about an employee's career aspirations when they were headed out the door.

The team needed to find a new way to make sure employees felt valued, engaged and heard. In other words, managers needed to do a better job of showing the love to their employees.

VP of HR Erin Earle joined forces with LinkedIn's head of engineering Kevin Scott to do just that. Together they set out on a mission to assess top talent across the company's engineering and operations teams, understand the flight risk of this group and develop plans to make sure they stayed. The Love Bus Tour was born.

"The Love Bus Tour was being rooted in the art and science of motivation and developed by members of the engineering HR business partner team (HRBP)," explains Erin.

"The thinking was that if senior leaders had coordinated skip-level conversations with top engineers to recognize their contributions and understand their aspirations, and then take actions accordingly, then those employees would 'feel the love' and become more excited about their future at LinkedIn and less likely to leave." In other words, by proactively having career conversations, they'd can get ahead of a person's decision to leave

By the end of 2015, the engineers who were part of this effort had an attrition rate of 8%, significantly lower than the rest of the engineering organization at 13%

In Kevin Scott's words, "We have amazing folks doing incredible work and we want to keep them. This conversation gave us the reminder that we need to constantly focus on listening to and learning from our teams to keep them engaged

The following year, the teams expanded this effort. They engaged more engineers and invested more heavily in training managers to lead retention conversations. Not only did participants have lower attrition compared to non-participants again (5.5% vs. 9.2%), but they reported significantly higher job satisfaction and manager effectiveness too

Identify program participants.

Get manager buy-in through in-person workshops and written communication.

Send personalized thank-you from head of engineering.

Facilitate conversations between top performing engineers and senior leaders.

Analyze conversations and develop personalized action plans.

We learned from the first year that we wanted to go deeper into why these conversations are so important. Our hypothesis was that if we focused on latest research on employee engagement and motivation, we could make the next training even more relevant and compelling to an engineering audience

We were able to see what was going on and what people were worried about at every level"

Once again, engineers who participated had lower attrition than those did not. Participants were leaving at a slower rate (-3.7%) compared to engineers who didn't participate and we saw an overall reduction in Engineering attrition.

Conclusion

What all we learned and understood is:

Why to Business face challenges to retain its staff?

Why retention is so important?

Why do you think employees leave?

Importance of Customer

Importance of Employee

Case Study

How to Retain talented employees? Or Reason for leaving organization

Motivation

How Google & LinkedIn worked to retain and engage its employees

John Rivers

Heike jung

Greg Giesen

Joy Hube

Jung H

Deborah laurel

Charles Creppy

ABOUT THE AUTHOR

Author has excellent knowledge in the field of Human Resource. Masters in Human Resource and further completed PG from IIM C – Indian Institute of Management Calcutta.
Love to motivated people and help them to achieve their dreams.

www.ingramcontent.com/pod-product-compliance
Lightning Source LLC
Chambersburg PA
CBHW070519220526
45467CB00002B/744